J 599.53 SPI
Spilsbury, Louise.
Dolphin

TE DUE

EAGLE PUBLIC LI
BOX 240 EAGLE
(970) 328-

EAGLE VALLEY LIBR

1 06 0005029412

D1075496

A Day in the Life: Sea Animals

Dolphin

Louise Spilsbury

Heinemann Library
Chicago, Illinois

www.heinemannraintree.com
Visit our website to find out
more information about
Heinemann-Raintree books.

To order:
☎ Phone 888-454-2279
🖳 Visit www.heinemannraintree.com
to browse our catalog and order online.

©2011 Heinemann Library
an imprint of Capstone Global Library, LLC
Chicago, Illinois

All rights reserved. No part of this publication may be
reproduced or transmitted in any form or by any means,
electronic or mechanica l, including photocopying,
recording, taping, or any information storage and retrieval
system, without permission in writing from the publisher.

Edited by Sian Smith, Nancy Dickmann, and
  Rebecca Rissman
Designed by Joanna Hinton-Malivoire
Picture research by Mica Brancic
Production by Victoria Fitzgerald
Originated by Capstone Global Library Ltd
Printed and bound in the United States of America,
  North Mankato, MN.

14 13 12 11 10
10 9 8 7 6 5 4 3 2

**Library of Congress Cataloging-in-
Publication Data**
Spilsbury, Louise.
  Dolphin / Louise Spilsbury.—1st ed.
    p.cm.—(A day in the life : sea animals)
  Includes bibliographical references and index.
  ISBN 978-1-4329-3999-1 (hc)
  ISBN 978-1-4329-4006-5 (pb)
1. Dolphins—Juvenile literature. I. Title.
  QL737.C432S57 2011
  599.53—dc22
                                2010000485
112010
005975RP

Acknowledgments

We would like to thank the following for permission to
reproduce photographs: Ardea p.18 (© Augusto Stanzani);
Corbis p.13 (Stuart Westmorland); FLPA pp.15 (Minden
Pictures/Flip Nicklin), 17 (Terry Whittaker); Image
Quest Marine pp.7, 21, 23: flipper (James D. Watt), 10
(V&W/Mark Conlin); Nature Picture Library p.16 (© Dan
Burton); Photolibrary pp.4 (imagebroker.net), 5 (Britain on
View/Splashdown Direct), 6 (Pacific Stock/Dave Fleetham),
8 (WaterFrame - Underwater Images/Reinhard Dirscherl),
9 (age fotostock/Fco Javier Gutierrez), 11 (Corbis), 12
(Oxford Scientific Films (OSF)/Splashdown Direct), 14
(WaterFrame - Underwater Images/Wolfgang Poelzer),
19 (Corbis), 23: breathe (Britain on View/Splashdown
Direct), 23: calf (Corbis), 23: dorsal fin (Oxford Scientific
Films (OSF)/Splashdown Direct), 23: pod (WaterFrame -
Underwater Images/Reinhard Dirscherl; Photoshot/NHPA)
pp.20, 23: surface (Annelene Oberholzer); Shutterstock
pp.22, 23: blowhole (Kristian Sekulic).

Cover photograph of a jumping dolphin reproduced
with permission of Corbis (© Image Source). Back cover
photograph of a blowhole reproduced with permission of
Shutterstock (© Kristian Sekulic). Back cover photograph
of teeth reproduced with permission of Corbis (© Stuart
Westmorland).

We would like to thank Michael Bright for his invaluable
help in the preparation of this book.

Every effort has been made to contact copyright holders
of material reproduced in this book. Any omissions will
be rectified in subsequent printings if notice is given to the
publisher.

All the Internet addresses (URLs) given in this book were
valid at the time of going to press. However, due to the
dynamic nature of the Internet, some addresses may have
changed, or sites may have changed or ceased to exist
since publication. While the author and publisher regret
any inconvenience this may cause readers, no responsibility
for any such changes can be accepted by either the author
or the publisher.

EAGLE PUBLIC LIBRARY DIST.
BOX 240 EAGLE, CO 81631
(970) 328-8800

Contents

Some words are shown in bold, **like this**.
You can find them in the glossary on page 23.

What Is a Dolphin?

Dolphins are animals that live in oceans all over the world.

Dolphins can live close to land or swim far out in the ocean.

blowhole

Dolphins swim and feed in the ocean but they **breathe** air.

A dolphin breathes through a **blowhole** on its head.

What Do Dolphins Look Like?

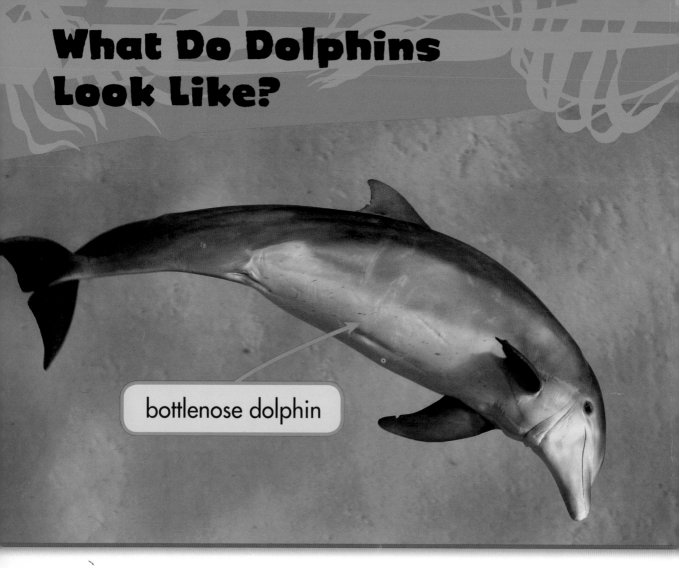

bottlenose dolphin

There are many different types of dolphin.

They may be black, white, gray, striped, or even spotted.

dorsal fin

flipper

tail

Bottlenose dolphins have curved **flippers**, a **dorsal fin**, and a tail.

They have a thick layer of fat under their skin to keep them warm.

What Do Dolphins Do All Day?

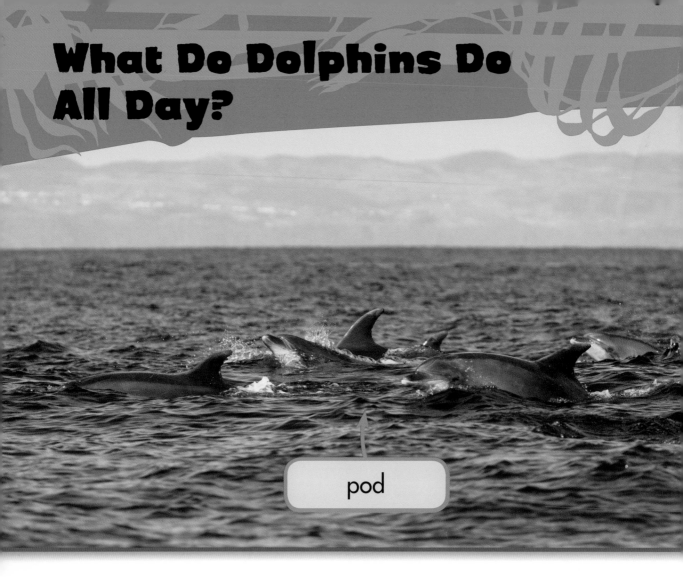

pod

Bottlenose dolphins mainly hunt for food in the morning and afternoon.

Dolphins live and hunt in groups called **pods**.

Dolphins squeak and grunt to tell each other things.

They also snap their mouths and smack the water with their tails.

How Do Dolphins Swim?

Dolphins move their tails up and down to swim forward.

They use their **flippers** to turn, steer, and stop.

Dolphins dive under the water to find food.

A bottlenose dolphin can hold its breath underwater for up to ten minutes.

What Do Dolphins Eat?

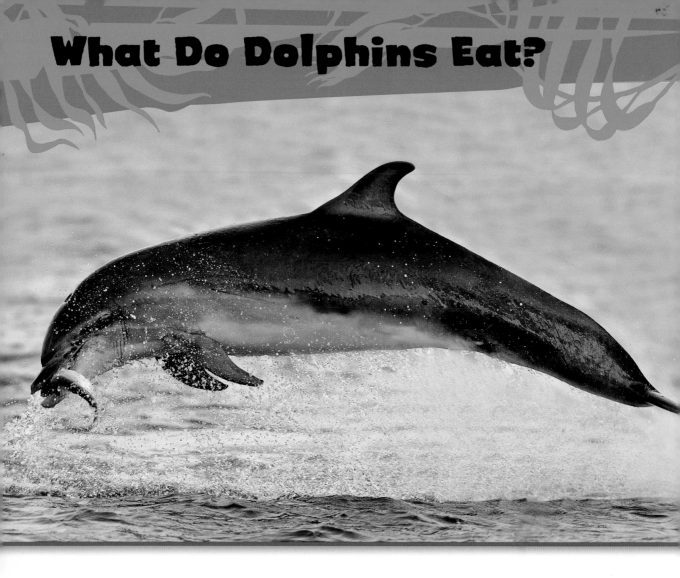

Dolphins eat small fish, squid, and shrimps.

Dolphins use their sharp teeth to grip slippery sea animals.

teeth

Dolphins do not use their teeth to chew or cut up their food.

They swallow their food whole.

How Do Dolphins Hunt?

Dolphins make sounds when they hunt.

The sounds bounce back and tell the dolphins where there is food to eat.

Bottlenose dolphins swim in circles around a group of fish.

They trap the fish and take turns to swim in and catch one.

When Do Dolphins Play?

In the day, dolphins often play together after they have eaten.

Playing helps dolphins learn hunting skills.

Dolphins race and chase each other.

They also jump out of the water and ride on waves.

What Are Dolphin Babies Like?

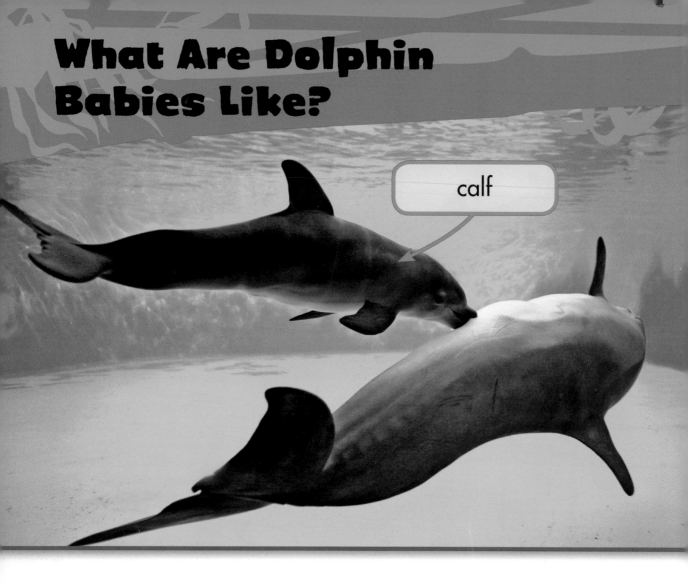

calf

A dolphin baby is called a **calf**.

A calf drinks milk from its mother's body.

A calf grows teeth to eat fish when it is about four months old.

A calf's mother and other dolphins teach it how to catch food.

What Do Dolphins Do at Night?

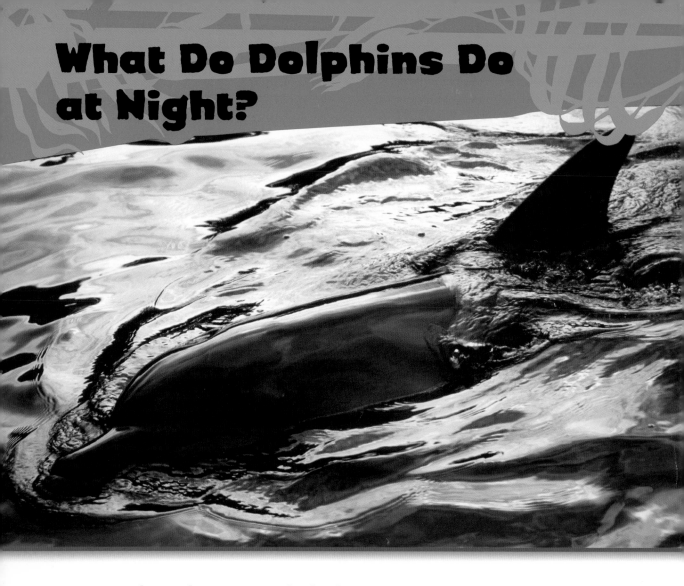

Many bottlenose dolphins rest at night.

They rest at the **surface** of the sea.

Dolphins cannot go into a deep sleep.

When dolphins rest, half their brain sleeps and the other half stays awake.

Dolphin Body Map

dorsal fin

blowhole

tail

flipper

eye

Glossary

 **blowhole** hole in the top of a dolphin's head for breathing

 **breathe** to take air into the body

 **calf** baby dolphin

 **dorsal fin** thin, flat part that sticks up from a dolphin's back

 **flipper** flat part of a dolphin's body that it uses for swimming

 **pod** group of dolphins

 **surface** top of the water

Find Out More

Books

Simon, Seymour. *Dolphins*. Washington, D.C.: Smithsonian Institution, 2009.

Stewart, Melissa. *Dolphins* (National Geographic Readers). Des Moines, Iowa: National Geographic Children's Books, 2010.

Websites

Watch a video on bottlenose dolphins and find out about them at: **kids. nationalgeographic.com/Animals/CreatureFeature/Bottlenose-dolphin**

Listen to the noises different dolphins make at: **seaworld.org/animal-info/ sound-library/index.htm**

Index